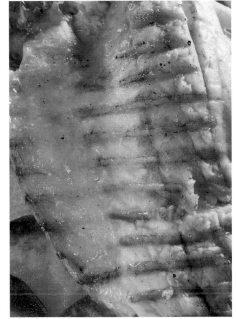

Quick & Simple

If you are looking for a fish dish that is really quick and easy to prepare, but is packed full of flavour, then take a look at the mouthwatering list below.

Tasty Main Courses

Fish comes in all shapes, sizes, textures and flavours. It is also really versatile and can be used to make delicious, healthy and varied meals for your family.

48 Tips & Hints for Fish & Seafood

FLAME TREE has been creating family-friendly, classic and beginner recipes for our bestselling cookbooks for over 12 years now. Our mission is to offer you a wide range of expert-tested dishes, while providing clear images of the final dish so that you can match it to your own results. We hope you enjoy this super selection of recipes – there are plenty more to try! Titles in this series include:

Cupcakes • Slow Cooker • Curries Chinese • Soups • Baking Breads Cakes • Simple Suppers • Pasta Chicken • Fish & Seafood • Chocolate

For more information please visit:
www.flametreepublishing.com

Smoked Salmon with Broad Beans & Rice

INGREDIENTS

Serves 4

2 tbsp sunflower oil

25 g/1 oz unsalted butter

1 onion, peeled and chopped

2 garlic cloves, peeled and chopped

175 g/6 oz asparagus tips, halved

75 g/3 oz frozen broad beans

150 ml/¼ pint dry white wine

125 g/4 oz sun-dried tomatoes, drained and sliced

125 g/4 oz baby spinach leaves, washed

450 g/1 lb cooked long-grain rice

3 tbsp crème fraîche

225 g/8 oz smoked salmon, cut into strips

75 g/3 oz freshly grated Parmesan cheese

salt and freshly ground black pepper

1   Heat a large wok, then add the oil and butter and, when melted, stir-fry the onion for 3 minutes, until almost softened. Add the garlic and asparagus tips and stir-fry for 3 minutes. Add the broad beans and wine and bring to the boil, then simmer, stirring occasionally, until the wine is reduced slightly.

2   Add the sun-dried tomatoes and bring back to the boil, then simmer for 2 minutes. Stir in the baby spinach leaves and cooked rice and return to the boil. Stir-fry for 2 minutes, or until the spinach is wilted and the rice is heated through thoroughly.

3   Stir in the crème fraîche, smoked salmon strips and Parmesan cheese. Stir well and cook, stirring frequently, until piping hot. Season to taste with salt and pepper. Serve immediately.

Rice with Smoked Salmon & Ginger

INGREDIENTS

Serves 4

225 g/8 oz basmati rice

600 ml/1 pint fish stock

1 bunch spring onions, trimmed and diagonally sliced

3 tbsp freshly chopped coriander

1 tsp grated fresh root ginger

200 g/7 oz sliced smoked salmon

2 tbsp soy sauce

1 tsp sesame oil

2 tsp lemon juice

4–6 slices pickled ginger

2 tsp sesame seeds

rocket leaves, to serve

FOOD FACT

Good smoked salmon should look moist and firm and have a peachy pink colour. If you buy it from a delicatessen counter, ask for it to be freshly sliced as any that has already been sliced may be dried out. Vacuum-packed salmon will keep for about 2 weeks in the refrigerator (check the use-by date), but once opened should be used within 3 days.

1 Place the rice in a sieve and rinse under cold water until the water runs clear. Drain, then place in a large saucepan with the stock and bring gently to the boil. Reduce to a simmer and cover with a tight-fitting lid. Cook for 10 minutes, then remove from the heat and leave, covered, for a further 10 minutes.

2 Stir the spring onions, coriander and fresh ginger into the cooked rice and mix well.

3 Spoon the rice into four tartlet tins, each measuring 10 cm/4 inches, and press down firmly with the back of a spoon to form cakes. Invert a tin onto an individual serving plate, then tap the base firmly and remove the tin. Repeat with the rest of the filled tins.

4 Top the rice with the salmon, folding if necessary, so the sides of the rice can still be seen in places. Mix together the soy sauce, sesame oil and lemon juice to make a dressing, then drizzle over the salmon. Top with the pickled ginger and a sprinkling of sesame seeds. Scatter the rocket leaves around the edge of the plates and serve immediately.

3

3

4

Fresh Tuna Salad

INGREDIENTS

Serves 4

225 g/8 oz mixed salad leaves
225 g/8 oz baby cherry tomatoes,
  halved lengthways
125 g/4 oz rocket leaves, washed
2 tbsp groundnut oil
550 g/1¼ lb boned tuna steaks,
  each cut into 4 small pieces
50 g/2 oz piece fresh
  Parmesan cheese

For the dressing:

8 tbsp olive oil
grated zest and juice of
  2 small lemons
1 tbsp wholegrain mustard
salt and freshly ground
  black pepper

HELPFUL HINT

Bags of mixed salad leaves can be bought from virtually all the major supermarkets. Although they may seem expensive, there is very little waste and they can save you time. Rinse the leaves before using.

1 Wash the salad leaves and place in a large salad bowl with the cherry tomatoes and rocket and reserve.

2 Heat the wok, then add the oil and heat until almost smoking. Add the tuna, skin-side down, and cook for 4–6 minutes, turning once during cooking, or until cooked and the flesh flakes easily. Remove from the heat and leave to stand in the juices for 2 minutes before removing.

3 Meanwhile make the dressing, place the olive oil, lemon zest and juices and mustard in a small bowl, or screw-topped jar, and whisk or shake well until well blended. Season to taste with salt and pepper.

4 Transfer the tuna to a clean chopping board and flake, then add it to the salad and toss lightly.

5 Using a swivel blade vegetable peeler, peel the piece of Parmesan cheese into shavings. Divide the salad between four large serving plates, drizzle the dressing over the salad, then scatter with the Parmesan shavings.

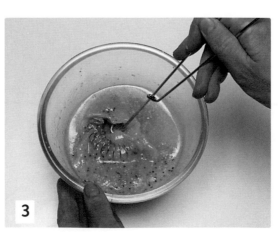

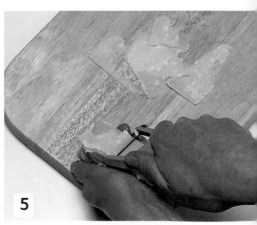

Pasta Provençale

INGREDIENTS

Serves 4

2 tbsp olive oil

1 garlic clove, peeled and crushed

1 onion, peeled and finely chopped

1 small fennel bulb, trimmed and
halved and thinly sliced

400 g can chopped tomatoes

1 rosemary sprig, plus extra sprig
to garnish

350 g/12 oz monkfish, skinned

2 tsp lemon juice

400 g/14 oz gnocchi pasta

50 g/2 oz pitted black olives

200 g can flageolet beans, drained
and rinsed

1 tbsp freshly chopped oregano, plus
sprig to garnish

salt and freshly ground black pepper

1 Heat the olive oil in a large saucepan, add the garlic and onion and cook gently for 5 minutes. Add the fennel and cook for a further 5 minutes. Stir in the chopped tomatoes and rosemary sprig. Half-cover the pan and simmer for 10 minutes.

2 Cut the monkfish into bite-sized pieces and sprinkle with the lemon juice. Add to the tomatoes, cover and simmer gently for 5 minutes, or until the fish is opaque.

3 Meanwhile, bring a large pan of lightly salted water to a rolling boil. Add the pasta and cook according to the packet instructions, or until 'al dente'. Drain the pasta thoroughly and return to the saucepan.

4 Remove the rosemary from the tomato sauce. Stir in the black olives, flageolet beans and chopped oregano, then season to taste with salt and pepper. Add the sauce to the pasta and toss gently together to coat, taking care not to break up the monkfish. Tip into a warmed serving bowl. Garnish with rosemary and oregano sprigs and serve immediately.

Salmon with Strawberry Sauce

INGREDIENTS

Serves 4

4 x 150 g/5 oz salmon fillets
25 g/1 oz butter
2 tbsp groundnut oil
1 dessert apple, cored and
 cut into chunks
1 bunch spring onions, trimmed
 and diagonally sliced
1 garlic clove, peeled and sliced
50 g/2 oz pine nuts
juice of 1 lemon
125 g/4 oz strawberries, hulled
 and halved
1 bunch basil, freshly chopped
salt and freshly ground black pepper

To serve:
freshly cooked creamy
 mashed potatoes
freshly cooked broad beans

HELPFUL HINT

This unusual choice of fruit sauce provides much-needed sharpness against the richness of the fish. Try not to overcook the strawberries or they will start to lose their shape and texture.

1 Wash the salmon fillets and pat dry on absorbent kitchen paper. Heat the wok, then add the butter and half the oil and heat until bubbling. Cook the salmon fillets flesh-side down for 5 minutes, until they are sealed. Then, using a fish slice, carefully turn the salmon fillets over and cook for a further 3–5 minutes, until the salmon flesh is just flaking.

2 Transfer the salmon fillets to warmed serving plates and keep warm in a low oven. Wipe the wok clean, then add the remaining oil to the wok and heat until almost smoking.

3 Add the apple chunks, spring onions, garlic slices and pine nuts and cook for 5 minutes, stirring occasionally, until they are golden brown.

4 Stir in the lemon juice, strawberries, chopped basil and season to taste with salt and pepper. Heat through thoroughly.

5 Spoon the sauce over the salmon fillets and serve immediately with creamy mashed potatoes and freshly cooked broad beans.

Spicy Cod Rice

INGREDIENTS

Serves 4

1 tbsp plain flour

1 tbsp freshly chopped coriander

1 tsp ground cumin

1 tsp ground coriander

550 g/1¼ lb thick-cut cod fillet,
  skinned and cut into large chunks

4 tbsp groundnut oil

50 g/2 oz cashew nuts

1 bunch spring onions, trimmed and
  diagonally sliced

1 red chilli, deseeded and chopped

1 carrot, peeled and cut
  into matchsticks

125 g/4 oz frozen peas

450 g/1 lb cooked long-grain rice

2 tbsp sweet chilli sauce

2 tbsp soy sauce

HELPFUL HINT

Care is needed when frying nuts as they have a tendency to turn from golden to burnt very quickly. An alternative is to toast them on a baking sheet in the oven at 180°C/350°F/Gas Mark 4 for about 5 minutes until they are golden and fragrant.

1 Mix together the flour, coriander, cumin and ground coriander on a large plate. Coat the cod in the spice mixture then place on a baking sheet, cover and chill in the refrigerator for 30 minutes.

2 Heat a large wok, then add 2 tablespoons of the oil and heat until almost smoking. Stir-fry the cashew nuts for 1 minute, until browned, then remove and reserve.

3 Add a further 1 tablespoon of the oil and heat until almost smoking. Add the cod and stir-fry for 2 minutes. Using a fish slice, turn the cod pieces over and cook for a further 2 minutes, until golden. Remove from the wok, place on a warm plate, cover and keep warm.

4 Add the remaining oil to the wok, heat until almost smoking then stir-fry the spring onions and chilli for 1 minute before adding the carrots and peas and stir-frying for a further 2 minutes. Stir in the rice, chilli sauce, soy sauce and cashew nuts and stir-fry for 3 more minutes. Add the cod, heat for 1 minute, then serve immediately.

Tagliatelle with Tuna & Anchovy Tapenade

INGREDIENTS

Serves 4

400 g/14 oz tagliatelle
125 g can tuna fish in oil, drained
45 g/1³/₄ oz can anchovy
  fillets, drained
150 g/5 oz pitted black olives
2 tbsp capers in brine, drained
2 tsp lemon juice
100 ml/3¹/₂ fl oz olive oil
2 tbsp freshly chopped parsley
freshly ground black pepper
sprigs of flat-leaf parsley, to garnish

FOOD FACT

Capers are the flower buds of the caper bush, which grows all over the Mediterranean region. The buds are picked before they open and preserved in vinegar and salt. The word tapenade (a mixture of capers, olives and fish, usually anchovies, pounded to a paste with olive oil) comes from the Provençal word for capers – tapeno.

1 Bring a large pan of lightly salted water to a rolling boil. Add the tagliatelle and cook according to the packet instructions, or until 'al dente'.

2 Meanwhile, place the tuna fish, anchovy fillets, olives and capers in a food processor, with the lemon juice and 2 tablespoons of the olive oil, and blend for a few seconds until roughly chopped.

3 With the motor running, pour in the remaining olive oil in a steady stream; the resulting mixture should be slightly chunky rather than smooth.

4 Spoon the sauce into a bowl, stir in the chopped parsley and season to taste with black pepper. Check the taste of the sauce and add a little more lemon juice, if required.

5 Drain the pasta thoroughly. Pour the sauce into the pan and cook over a low heat for 1–2 minutes to warm through.

6 Return the drained pasta to the pan and mix together with the sauce. Tip into a warmed serving bowl or spoon on to warm individual plates. Garnish with sprigs of flat-leaf parsley and serve immediately.

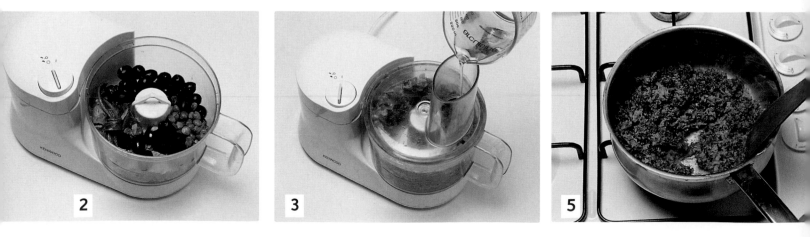

2 3 5

Sardines with Redcurrants

INGREDIENTS

Serves 4

2 tbsp redcurrant jelly
finely grated rind of 1 lime
2 tbsp medium dry sherry
450 g/1 lb fresh sardines, cleaned and
  heads removed
sea salt and freshly ground
  black pepper
lime wedges, to garnish

To serve:

fresh redcurrants
fresh green salad

COOK'S TIP

Most fish are sold cleaned but it is quite easy to do yourself. Using the back of a knife, scrape off the scales from the tail towards the head. Make a small slit along the bellies of the fish using a sharp knife. Carefully scrape out the entrails and rinse thoroughly under cold running water. Pat dry with absorbent paper.

1 Preheat the grill and line the grill rack with tinfoil 2–3 minutes before cooking.

2 Warm the redcurrant jelly in a bowl standing over a pan of gently simmering water and stir until smooth. Add the lime rind and sherry to the bowl and stir well until blended.

3 Lightly rinse the sardines and pat dry with absorbent kitchen paper.

4 Place on a chopping board and with a sharp knife make several diagonal cuts across the flesh of each fish. Season the sardines inside the cavities with salt and pepper.

5 Gently brush the warm marinade over the skin and inside the cavities of the sardines.

6 Place on the grill rack and cook under the preheated grill for 8–10 minutes, or until the fish are cooked.

7 Carefully turn the sardines over at least once during grilling. Baste occasionally with the remaining redcurrant and lime marinade. Garnish with the redcurrants. Serve immediately with the salad and lime wedges.

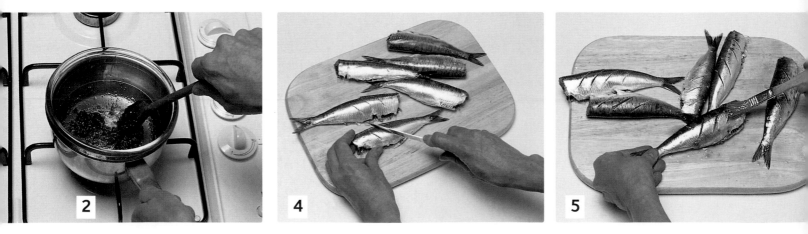

Salmon & Filo Parcels

INGREDIENTS

Serves 4

1 tbsp sunflower oil
1 bunch of spring onions, trimmed
   and finely chopped
1 tsp paprika
175 g/6 oz long-grain white rice
300 ml/½ pint fish stock
salt and freshly ground black pepper
450 g/1 lb salmon fillet, cubed
1 tbsp freshly chopped parsley
grated rind and juice of 1 lemon
150 g/5 oz rocket
150 g/5 oz spinach
12 sheets filo pastry
50 g/2 oz butter, melted

1   Preheat the oven to 200°C/400°F/Gas Mark 6. Heat the oil in a small frying pan and gently cook the spring onions for 2 minutes. Stir in the paprika and continue to cook for 1 minute, then remove from the heat and reserve.

2   Put the rice in a sieve and rinse under cold running water until the water runs clear; drain. Put the rice and stock in a saucepan, bring to the boil, then cover and simmer for 10 minutes, or until the liquid is absorbed and the rice is tender. Add the spring onion mixture and fork through. Season to taste with salt and pepper, then leave to cool.

3   In a non-metallic bowl, mix together the salmon, parsley, lemon rind and juice and salt and pepper. Reserve.

4   Blanch the rocket and spinach for 30 seconds in a large saucepan of boiling water, or until just wilted. Drain well in a colander and refresh in plenty of cold water, then squeeze out as much moisture as possible.

5   Brush three sheets of filo pastry with melted butter and lay them on top of one another. Take a quarter of the rice mixture and arrange it in an oblong in the centre of the pastry. On top of this place a quarter of the salmon followed by a quarter of the rocket and spinach.

6   Draw up the pastry around the filling and twist at the top to create a parcel. Repeat with the remaining pastry and filling until you have four parcels. Brush with the remaining butter.

7   Place the parcels on a lightly oiled baking tray and cook in the preheated oven for 20 minutes, or until golden brown and cooked. Serve immediately.

Salmon Teriyaki with Noodles & Crispy Greens

INGREDIENTS

Serves 4

350 g/12 oz salmon fillet
3 tbsp Japanese soy sauce
3 tbsp mirin or sweet sherry
3 tbsp sake
1 tbsp freshly grated root ginger
225 g/8 oz spring greens
groundnut oil for deep-frying
pinch of salt
½ tsp caster sugar
125 g/4 oz cellophane noodles

To garnish:

1 tbsp freshly chopped dill
sprigs of fresh dill
zest of ½ lemon

1   Cut the salmon into paper-thin slices and place in a shallow dish. Mix together the soy sauce, mirin or sherry, sake and the ginger. Pour over the salmon, cover and leave to marinate for 15–30 minutes.

2   Remove and discard the thick stalks from the spring greens. Lay several leaves on top of each other, roll up tightly, then shred finely.

3   Pour in enough oil to cover about 5 cm/2 inches of the wok. Deep-fry the greens in batches for about 1 minute each until crisp. Remove and drain on absorbent kitchen paper. Transfer to a serving dish, sprinkle with salt and sugar and toss together.

4   Place the noodles in a bowl and pour over warm water to cover. Leave to soak for 15–20 minutes until soft, then drain. With scissors cut into 15 cm/6 inch lengths.

5   Preheat the grill. Remove the salmon slices from the marinade, reserving the marinade for later, and arrange them in a single layer on a baking sheet. Grill for about 2 minutes, until lightly cooked, without turning.

6   When the oil in the wok is cool enough, tip most of it away, leaving about 1 tablespoon behind. Heat until hot, then add the noodles and the reserved marinade and stir-fry for 3–4 minutes. Tip the noodles into a large warmed serving bowl and arrange the salmon slices on top, garnished with chopped dill, sprigs of fresh dill and lemon zest. Scatter with a little of the crispy greens and serve the rest separately.

Barbecued Fish Kebabs

INGREDIENTS

Serves 4

450 g/1 lb herring or mackerel fillets,
  cut into chunks
2 small red onions, peeled
  and quartered
16 cherry tomatoes
salt and freshly ground black pepper

For the sauce:

150 ml /¼ pint fish stock
5 tbsp tomato ketchup
2 tbsp Worcestershire sauce
2 tbsp wine vinegar
2 tbsp brown sugar
2 drops tabasco
2 tbsp tomato purée

TASTY TIP

Instead of cooking indoors, cook these kebabs on the barbecue for a delicious charcoaled flavour. Light the barbecue at least 20 minutes before use in order to allow the coals to heat up. The coals will have a grey-white ash when ready. Barbecue some peppers and red onions and serve with a mixed salad as an accompaniment to the fish kebabs.

1 Line a grill rack with a single layer of tinfoil and preheat the grill at a high temperature, 2 minutes before use.

2 If using wooden skewers, soak in cold water for 30 minutes to prevent them from catching fire during cooking.

3 Meanwhile, prepare the sauce. Add the fish stock, tomato ketchup, Worcestershire sauce, vinegar, sugar, tabasco and tomato purée to a small saucepan. Stir well and leave to simmer for 5 minutes.

4 When ready to cook, drain the skewers, if necessary, then thread the fish chunks, the quartered red onions and the cherry tomatoes alternately on to the skewers.

5 Season the kebabs to taste with salt and pepper and brush with the sauce. Grill under the preheated grill for 8–10 minutes, basting with the sauce occasionally during cooking. Turn the kebabs often to ensure that they are cooked thoroughly and evenly on all sides. Serve immediately with couscous.

3

4

5

Salmon Fish Cakes

INGREDIENTS

Serves 4

450 g/1 lb salmon fillet, skinned

salt and freshly ground black pepper

450 g/1 lb potatoes, peeled and cut
  into chunks

25 g/1 oz butter

1 tbsp milk

2 medium tomatoes, skinned,
  deseeded and chopped

2 tbsp freshly chopped parsley

75 g/3 oz wholemeal breadcrumbs

25 g/1 oz Cheddar cheese, grated

2 tbsp plain flour

2 medium eggs, beaten

3–4 tbsp vegetable oil

To serve:

ready-made raita

sprigs of fresh mint

HELPFUL HINT

To remove the skins from the tomatoes, pierce each with the tip of a sharp knife, then plunge into boiling water and leave for up to 1 minute. Drain, then rinse in cold water – the skins should peel off easily.

1 Place the salmon in a shallow frying pan and cover with water. Season to taste with salt and pepper and simmer for 8–10 minutes until the fish is cooked. Drain and flake into a bowl.

2 Boil the potatoes in lightly salted water until soft, then drain. Mash with the butter and milk until smooth. Add the potato to the bowl of fish and stir in the tomatoes and half the parsley. Adjust the seasoning to taste. Chill the mixture in the refrigerator for at least 2 hours to firm up.

3 Mix the breadcrumbs with the grated cheese and the remaining parsley. When the fish mixture is firm, form into eight flat cakes. First, lightly coat the fish cakes in the flour, then dip into the beaten egg, allowing any excess to drip back into the bowl. Finally, press into the breadcrumb mixture until well coated.

4 Heat a little of the oil in a frying pan and fry the fish cakes in batches for 2–3 minutes on each side until golden and crisp, adding more oil if necessary. Serve with raita garnished with sprigs of mint.

Salmon Noisettes with Fruity Sauce

INGREDIENTS

Serves 4

4 x 125 g/4 oz salmon steaks
grated rind and juice of 2 lemons
grated rind and juice of 1 lime
3 tbsp olive oil
1 tbsp clear honey
1 tbsp wholegrain mustard
coarse sea salt and freshly ground
  black pepper
1 tbsp groundnut oil
125 g/4 oz mixed salad
  leaves, washed
1 bunch watercress, washed and
  thick stalks removed
250 g/9 oz baby plum
  tomatoes, halved

HELPFUL HINT

When choosing salad leaves for this dish, look out for slightly bitter leaves such as frisée and radicchio, which will stand up well to the heat of the salmon and contrast well with the sweetness of the sauce.

1 Using a sharp knife, cut the bone away from each salmon steak to create 2 salmon fillets. Repeat with the remaining salmon steaks. Shape the salmon fillets into noisettes and secure with fine string.

2 Mix together the citrus rinds and juices, olive oil, honey, wholegrain mustard, salt and pepper in a shallow dish. Add the salmon fillets and turn to coat. Cover and leave to marinate in the refrigerator for 4 hours, turning them occasionally in the marinade.

3 Heat the wok then add the groundnut oil and heat until hot. Lift out the salmon noisettes, reserving the marinade. Add the salmon to the wok and cook for 6–10 minutes, turning once during cooking, until cooked and the fish is just flaking. Pour the marinade into the wok and heat through gently.

4 Mix together the salad leaves, watercress and tomatoes and arrange on serving plates. Top with the salmon noisettes and drizzle over any remaining warm marinade. Serve immediately.

Cod with Fennel & Cardamom

INGREDIENTS

Serves 4

1 garlic clove, peeled
and crushed
finely grated rind of 1 lemon
1 tsp lemon juice
1 tbsp olive oil
1 fennel bulb
1 tbsp cardamom pods
salt and freshly ground
black pepper
4 x 175 g/6 oz thick cod fillets

FOOD FACT

When buying fresh fish, look out for fish that does not smell. Any fish that smells of ammonia should be avoided. The flesh of the fish should be plump and firm-looking. The eyes should be bright, not sunken. If in doubt, choose frozen fish. This is cleaned and packed almost as soon as it is caught. It is often fresher and contains more nutrients than its fresh counterparts.

1 Preheat the oven to 190°C/375°F/Gas Mark 5. Place the garlic in a small bowl with the lemon rind, juice and olive oil and stir well.

2 Cover and leave to infuse for at least 30 minutes. Stir well before using.

3 Trim the fennel bulb, thinly slice and place in a bowl.

4 Place the cardamom pods in a pestle and mortar and lightly pound to crack the pods.

5 Alternatively place in a polythene bag and pound gently with a rolling pin. Add the crushed cardamom to the fennel slices.

6 Season the fish with salt and pepper and place on to four separate 20.5 x 20.5 cm/8 x 8 inch parchment paper squares.

7 Spoon the fennel mixture over the fish and drizzle with the infused oil.

8 Place the parcels on a baking sheet and bake in the preheated oven for 8–10 minutes or until cooked. Serve immediately in the paper parcels.

Chunky Halibut Casserole

INGREDIENTS

Serves 6

50 g/2 oz butter or margarine

2 large onions, peeled and sliced
  into rings

1 red pepper, deseeded and
  roughly chopped

450 g/1 lb potatoes, peeled

450 g/1 lb courgettes, trimmed
  and thickly sliced

2 tbsp plain flour

1 tbsp paprika

2 tsp vegetable oil

300 ml/½ pint white wine

150 ml/¼ pint fish stock

400 g can chopped tomatoes

2 tbsp freshly chopped basil

salt and freshly ground black pepper

450 g/1 lb halibut fillet, skinned and
  cut into 2.5 cm/ 1 inch cubes

sprigs of fresh basil, to garnish

freshly cooked rice, to serve

1   Melt the butter or margarine in a large saucepan, add the onions and pepper and cook for 5 minutes, or until softened.

2   Cut the peeled potatoes into 2.5 cm/1 inch dice, rinse lightly and shake dry, then add them to the onions and pepper in the saucepan. Add the courgettes and cook, stirring frequently, for a further 2–3 minutes.

3   Sprinkle the flour, paprika and vegetable oil into the saucepan and cook, stirring continuously, for 1 minute. Pour in 150 ml/¼ pint of the wine, with all the stock and the chopped tomatoes, and bring to the boil.

4   Add the basil to the casserole, season to taste with salt and pepper and cover. Simmer for 15 minutes, then add the halibut and the remaining wine and simmer very gently for a further 5–7 minutes, or until the fish and vegetables are just tender. Garnish with basil sprigs and serve immediately with freshly cooked rice.

1

3

4

Chinese Steamed Sea Bass with Black Beans

INGREDIENTS

Serves 4

1.1 kg/2½ lb sea bass, cleaned with
head and tail left on

1–2 tbsp rice wine or dry sherry

1½ tbsp groundnut oil

2–3 tbsp fermented black beans,
rinsed and drained

1 garlic clove, peeled and
finely chopped

1 cm/½ inch piece fresh root ginger,
peeled and finely chopped

4 spring onions, trimmed and thinly
sliced diagonally

2–3 tbsp soy sauce

125 ml/4 fl oz fish or chicken stock

1–2 tbsp sweet Chinese chilli sauce,
or to taste

2 tsp sesame oil

sprigs of fresh coriander, to garnish

1 Using a sharp knife, cut three or four deep diagonal slashes along both sides of the fish. Sprinkle the Chinese rice wine or sherry inside and over the fish and gently rub into the skin on both sides.

2 Lightly brush a heatproof plate large enough to fit into a large wok or frying pan with a little of the groundnut oil. Place the fish on the plate, curving the fish along the inside edge of the dish, then leave for 20 minutes.

3 Place a wire rack or inverted ramekin in the wok and pour in enough water to come about 2.5 cm/1 inch up the side. Bring to the boil over a high heat.

4 Carefully place the plate with the fish on the rack or ramekin, cover and steam for 12 15 minutes, or until the fish is tender and the flesh is opaque when pierced with a knife near the bone.

5 Remove the plate with the fish from the wok and keep warm. Remove the rack or ramekin from the wok and pour off the water. Return the wok to the heat, add the remaining groundnut oil and swirl to coat the bottom and side. Add the black beans, garlic and ginger and stir-fry for 1 minute.

6 Add the spring onions, soy sauce, fish or chicken stock and boil for 1 minute. Stir in the chilli sauce and sesame oil, then pour the sauce over the cooked fish. Garnish with coriander sprigs and serve immediately.

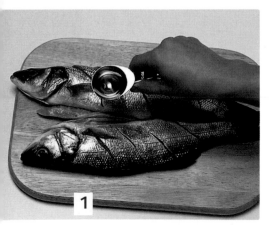
1

4

5

Potato Boulangere with Sea Bass

INGREDIENTS

Serves 2

450 g/1 lb potatoes, peeled and
   thinly sliced
1 large onion, peeled and thinly sliced
salt and freshly ground black pepper
300 ml/½ pint fish or vegetable stock
75 g/3 oz butter or margarine
350 g/12 oz sea bass fillets
sprigs of fresh flat leaf parsley,
   to garnish

1   Preheat the oven to 200°C/400°F/Gas Mark 6. Lightly grease a
    shallow 1.4 litre/2½ pint baking dish with oil or butter. Layer the
    potato slices and onions alternately in the prepared dish, seasoning
    each layer with salt and pepper.

2   Pour the stock over the top, then cut 50 g/2 oz of the butter or
    margarine into small pieces and dot over the top layer. Bake in the
    preheated oven for 50–60 minutes. Do not cover the dish at this stage.

3   Lightly rinse the sea bass fillets and pat dry on absorbent kitchen
    paper. Cook in a griddle, or heat the remaining butter or margarine
    in a frying pan and shallow fry the fish fillets for 3–4 minutes per
    side, flesh side first. Remove from the pan with a slotted spatula
    and drain on absorbent kitchen paper.

4   Remove the partly cooked potato and onion mixture from the oven
    and place the fish on the top. Cover with tinfoil and return to the
    oven for 10 minutes until heated through. Garnish with sprigs of
    parsley and serve immediately.

FOOD FACT

Sea bass, also known as sea perch, is a large round fish which grows up to 1 m/3⅓ ft long, and may weigh up to 9 kg/20 lb. In appearance, it is similar to a salmon, but is a much darker grey colour. Cook it gently and handle it with care, as the flesh is soft and delicate.

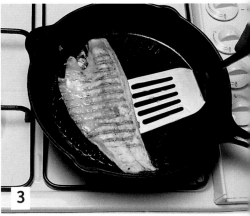

Grilled Red Mullet with Orange & Anchovy Sauce

INGREDIENTS

Serves 4

2 oranges

4 x 175 g/6 oz red mullet, cleaned
  and descaled

salt and freshly ground black pepper

4 sprigs of fresh rosemary

1 lemon, sliced

2 tbsp olive oil

2 garlic cloves, peeled and crushed

6 anchovy fillets in oil, drained and
  roughly chopped

2 tsp freshly chopped rosemary

1 tsp lemon juice

1 Preheat the grill and line the grill rack with tinfoil just before cooking. Peel the oranges with a sharp knife, over a bowl in order to catch the juice. Cut into thin slices and reserve. If necessary, make up the juice to 150 ml/¼ pint with extra juice.

2 Place the fish on a chopping board and make two diagonal slashes across the thickest part of both sides of the fish. Season well, both inside and out, with salt and pepper. Tuck a rosemary sprig and a few lemon slices inside the cavity of each fish. Brush the fish with a little of the olive oil and then cook under the preheated grill for 4–5 minutes on each side. The flesh should just fall away from the bone.

3 Heat the remaining oil in a saucepan and gently fry the garlic and anchovies for 3–4 minutes. Do not allow to brown. Add the chopped rosemary and plenty of black pepper. The anchovies will be salty enough, so do not add any salt. Stir in the orange slices with their juice and the lemon juice. Simmer gently until heated through. Spoon the sauce over the red mullet and serve immediately.

Seared Tuna with Pernod & Thyme

INGREDIENTS

Serves 4

4 tuna or swordfish steaks
salt and freshly ground black pepper
3 tbsp Pernod
1 tbsp olive oil
zest and juice of 1 lime
2 tsp fresh thyme leaves
4 sun-dried tomatoes

To serve:

freshly cooked mixed rice
tossed green salad

HELPFUL HINT

Tuna is now widely available all year round at many fishmongers and in supermarkets. Tuna is an oily fish rich in Omega-3 fatty acids, which help prevent heart disease by lowering blood cholesterol levels. Tuna is usually sold in steaks, and the flesh should be dark red in colour.

1 Wipe the fish steaks with a damp cloth or dampened kitchen paper.

2 Season both sides of the fish to taste with salt and pepper, then place in a shallow bowl and reserve.

3 Mix together the Pernod, olive oil, lime zest and juice with the fresh thyme leaves.

4 Finely chop the sun-dried tomatoes and add to the Pernod mixture.

5 Pour the Pernod mixture over the fish and chill in the refrigerator for about 2 hours, spooning the marinade occasionally over the fish.

6 Heat a griddle or heavy-based frying pan. Drain the fish, reserving the marinade. Cook the fish for 3–4 minutes on each side for a steak that is still slightly pink in the middle. Or, if liked, cook the fish for 1–2 minutes longer on each side if you prefer your fish cooked through.

7 Place the remaining marinade in a small saucepan and bring to the boil. Pour the marinade over the fish and serve immediately, with the mixed rice and salad.

Tuna & Mushroom Ragout

INGREDIENTS

Serves 4

225 g/8 oz basmati and wild rice
50 g/2 oz butter
1 tbsp olive oil
1 large onion, peeled and
   finely chopped
1 garlic clove, peeled and crushed
300 g/11 oz baby button mushrooms,
   wiped and halved
2 tbsp plain flour
400 g can chopped tomatoes
1 tbsp freshly chopped parsley
dash of Worcestershire sauce
400 g can tuna in oil, drained
salt and freshly ground black pepper
4 tbsp Parmesan cheese, grated
1 tbsp freshly shredded basil

To serve:
green salad
garlic bread

TASTY TIP
Fresh basil can be difficult to find
during the winter months. If you
have problems finding it, buy
chopped tomatoes that have basil
already added to them, or use extra
freshly chopped parsley instead.

1 Cook the basmati and wild rice in a saucepan of boiling salted water for 20 minutes, then drain and return to the pan. Stir in half of the butter, cover the pan and leave to stand for 2 minutes until all of the butter has melted.

2 Heat the oil and the remaining butter in a frying pan and cook the onion for 1–2 minutes until soft. Add the garlic and mushrooms and continue to cook for a further 3 minutes.

3 Stir in the flour and cook for 1 minute, then add the tomatoes and bring the sauce to the boil. Add the parsley, Worcestershire sauce and tuna and simmer gently for 3 minutes. Season to taste with salt and freshly ground pepper.

4 Stir the rice well, then spoon onto four serving plates and top with the tuna and mushroom mixture. Sprinkle with a spoonful of grated Parmesan cheese and some shredded basil for each portion and serve immediately with a green salad and chunks of garlic bread.

1

2

3

Fragrant Thai Swordfish with Peppers

INGREDIENTS

Serves 4–6

550 g/1¼ lb swordfish, cut into
  5 cm/2 inch strips
2 tbsp vegetable oil
2 lemon grass stalks, peeled, bruised
  and cut into 2.5 cm/1 inch pieces
2.5 cm/1 inch piece fresh root ginger,
  peeled and thinly sliced
4–5 shallots, peeled and thinly sliced
2–3 garlic cloves, peeled and
  thinly sliced
1 small red pepper, deseeded and
  thinly sliced
1 small yellow pepper, deseeded and
  thinly sliced
2 tbsp soy sauce
2 tbsp Chinese rice wine or dry sherry
1–2 tsp sugar
1 tsp sesame oil
1 tbsp Thai or Italian basil, shredded
salt and freshly ground black pepper
1 tbsp toasted sesame seeds

For the marinade:

1 tbsp soy sauce
1 tbsp Chinese rice wine or dry sherry
1 tbsp sesame oil
1 tbsp cornflour

1 Blend all the marinade ingredients together in a shallow, non-metallic baking dish. Add the swordfish and spoon the marinade over the fish. Cover and leave to marinate in the refrigerator for at least 30 minutes.

2 Using a slotted spatula or spoon, remove the swordfish from the marinade and drain briefly on absorbent kitchen paper. Heat a wok or large frying pan, add the oil and when hot, add the swordfish and stir-fry for 2 minutes, or until it begins to brown. Remove the swordfish and drain on absorbent kitchen paper.

3 Add the lemon grass, ginger, shallots and garlic to the wok and stir-fry for 30 seconds. Add the peppers, soy sauce, Chinese rice wine or sherry and sugar and stir-fry for 3–4 minutes.

4 Return the swordfish to the wok and stir-fry gently for 1–2 minutes, or until heated through and coated with the sauce. If necessary, moisten the sauce with a little of the marinade or some water. Stir in the sesame oil and the basil and season to taste with salt and pepper. Tip into a warmed serving bowl, sprinkle with sesame seeds and serve immediately.

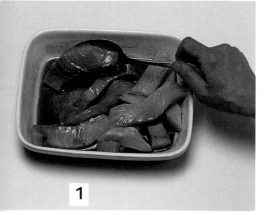

1

3

4

Scallops & Monkfish Kebabs with Fennel Sauce

INGREDIENTS

Serves 4

700 g/1½ lb monkfish tail
8 large fresh scallops
2 tbsp olive oil
1 garlic clove, peeled and crushed
freshly ground black pepper
1 fennel bulb, trimmed and
   thinly sliced
assorted salad leaves, to serve

For the sauce:

2 tbsp fennel seeds
pinch of chilli flakes
4 tbsp olive oil
2 tsp lemon juice
salt and freshly ground black pepper

1 Place the monkfish on a chopping board and remove the skin and the bone that runs down the centre of the tail and discard. Lightly rinse and pat dry with absorbent kitchen paper. Cut into 12 equal-sized pieces and place in a shallow bowl.

2 Remove the scallops from their shells, if necessary, and clean thoroughly discarding the black vein. Rinse lightly and pat dry with absorbent kitchen paper. Put in the bowl with the fish.

3 Blend the 2 tablespoons of olive oil, the crushed garlic and a pinch of black pepper in a small bowl, then pour the mixture over the monkfish and scallops, making sure they are well coated. Cover lightly and leave to marinate in the refrigerator for at least 30 minutes, or longer if time permits. Spoon over the marinade occasionally.

4 Lightly crush the fennel seeds and chilli flakes in a pestle and mortar. Stir in the 4 tablespoons of olive oil and lemon juice and season to taste with salt and pepper. Cover and leave to infuse for 20 minutes.

5 Drain the monkfish and scallops, reserving the marinade and thread on to four skewers.

6 Spray a griddle pan with a fine spray of oil, then heat until almost smoking and cook the kebabs for 5–6 minutes, turning halfway through and brushing with the marinade throughout.

7 Brush the fennel slices with the fennel sauce and cook on the griddle for 1 minute on each side. Serve the fennel slices, topped with the kebabs and drizzled with the fennel sauce. Serve with a few assorted salad leaves.

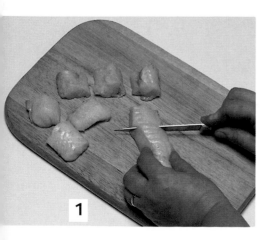

1

3

4

Fish Roulades with Rice & Spinach

INGREDIENTS

Serves 4

4 x 175 g/6 oz lemon sole, skinned

salt and freshly ground black pepper

1 tsp fennel seeds

75 g/3 oz long-grain rice, cooked

150 g/5 oz white crab meat, fresh
   or canned

125 g/4 oz baby spinach, washed
   and trimmed

5 tbsp dry white wine

5 tbsp half-fat crème fraîche

2 tbsp freshly chopped parsley, plus
   extra to garnish

asparagus spears, to serve

FOOD FACT

Spinach is one of the healthiest leafy green vegetables to be eaten. It also acts as an antioxidant and it is suggested that it can reduce the risk of certain cancers. Why not serve this dish with whole-grain rice to add nutritional value and to give it a nuttier taste.

1 Wipe each fish fillet with either a clean damp cloth or kitchen paper. Place on a chopping board, skinned-side up and season lightly with salt and black pepper.

2 Place the fennel seeds in a pestle and mortar and crush lightly. Transfer to a small bowl and stir in the cooked rice. Drain the crab meat thoroughly. Add to the rice mixture and mix lightly.

3 Lay 2–3 spinach leaves over each fillet and top with a quarter of the crab meat mixture. Roll up and secure with a cocktail stick if necessary. Place into a large pan and pour over the wine. Cover and cook on a medium heat for 5–7 minutes or until cooked.

4 Remove the fish from the cooking liquor, and transfer to a serving plate and keep warm. Stir the crème fraîche into the cooking liquor and season to taste. Heat for 3 minutes, then stir in the chopped parsley.

5 Spoon the sauce on to the base of a plate. Cut each roulade into slices and arrange on top of the sauce. Serve with freshly cooked asparagus spears.

2   3   4

Step-by-Step, Practical Recipes Fish & Seafood: Tips & Hints

 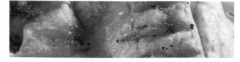 

Tasty Tip

Anchovies are mature sardines. They are heavily salted after filleting to preserve them, so should only be used in small quantities. Because they are so full of flavour, they are great for adding to sauces (see p14 and 36). For a slightly less salty dish, drain the anchovies and soak in a little milk for about 20 minutes before using.

Helpful Hint

Cooking fish in parchment paper parcels (see p28) is an excellent way of keeping in all the juices, flavour and aroma of the fish and vegetables. Your guests will also enjoy the anticipation of opening these surprise packages. Do let the parcels stand for a few minutes before serving as the steam can be burning hot when opened.

Food Fact

Halibut is a flatfish with firm, milky white flesh that has an almost meaty texture, making it ideal for a casserole (see p30). They can grow to an enormous size, at times weighing in at over 200 kg/ 444 lb, and are fished in the deep, freezing-cold waters of the North Sea.

Food Fact

Two varieties of smoked trout are generally available. One type resembles smoked salmon in colour, texture and flavour, and can be cut into thin slivers. Equally delicious is hot smoked rainbow trout, which is available as a whole fish or in fillets. These should be skinned and the bones should be removed before use. The flesh can then be broken into large flakes. Smoked trout is fairly salty, so any sauce for the fish requires a minimal amount of seasoning with salt.

Helpful Hint

When grilling fish, line the grill pan with tin foil to help catch any of the juices as the fish cooks. The best tasting dishes can require simply brushing the fish with olive oil and seasoning with salt and pepper, or some carefully chosen herbs. Making three slashes across the fish before you grill it will also add flavour.

Tasty Tip

Eat clams within 24 hours of buying them to enjoy them at their best. To make sure they are sweet and tender, steam the clams until the shells have just opened, as overcooking will toughen them.

Helpful Hint

Some fishmongers still sell mussels by volume rather than weight: 1.1 litres/2 pints is the equivalent of 900 g/2 lb. If you are not cooking mussels within a few hours of buying them, store in a bowl of water in a cold place.

Food Fact

A terrific complement to fish dishes are two types of sesame oil – the pale, light version, made from untoasted seeds, and the rich, dark kind, made from toasted seeds. The latter has a very strong, nutty flavour that can be overpowering in large quantities. It might be a good idea to dilute it, 1 tbsp to 1 tbsp of sunflower oil.

Food Fact

Mackerel is a relatively cheap fish and one of the richest sources of minerals, oils and vitamins available. Combined with salads, it is a cheap way to incorporate many essential nutrients into your diet.

Tasty Tip

Serving mussels in their shells with a delicious sauce is a fantastic way to eat them. The shells can be used to scoop up the sauce, adding flavour to every mouthful. Clams, which have a sweeter flavour, can be served in the same way.

Helpful Hint

Oily fish, such as sardines, mackerel and tuna have a higher fat content than white fish. They are an excellent source of Omega-3 polyunsaturated fatty acids, important in fighting heart disease, cancers and arthritis, and often have a deliciously robust flavour.

Food Fact

Shrimp paste is made from fermented, salted shrimp purée that has been dried in the sun. It should be blended with a little water before use. Shrimp sauce, which is not dried, makes a good substitute.

First published in 2012 by
FLAME TREE PUBLISHING LTD
Crabtree Hall, Crabtree Lane, Fulham, London, SW6 6TY, United Kingdom
www.flametreepublishing.com

The CIP record for this book is available from the British Library • Printed in China

NOTE: Recipes using uncooked eggs should be avoided by infants, the elderly, pregnant women and anyone suffering from an illness.

18 17 16 15 14 13 12   10 9 8 7 6 5 4 3 2 1

ISBN: 978-0-85775-613-8

ACKNOWLEDGEMENTS: Authors: Catherine Atkinson, Juliet Barker, Gina Steer, Vicki Smallwood, Carol Tennant, Mari Mererid Williams, Elizabeth Wolf-Cohen and Simone Wright. Photography: Colin Bowling, Paul Forrester and Stephen Brayne. Home Economists and Stylists: Jacqueline Bellefontaine, Mandy Phipps, Vicki Smallwood and Penny Stephens. All props supplied by Barbara Stewart at Surfaces. Publisher and Creative Director: Nick Wells. Editorial: Catherine Taylor, Sarah Goulding, Marcus Hardie, Gina Steer and Karen Fitzpatrick. Design and Production: Chris Herbert, Mike Spender, Colin Rudderham and Helen Wall.